best
easy
day hikes
Santa Fe

Linda and Katie Regnier

FALCON®

GUILFORD, CONNECTICUT
AN IMPRINT OF THE GLOBE PEQUOT PRESS

AFALCONGUIDE®

Copyright © 1999 by The Globe Pequot Press
Previously published by Falcon Publishing, Inc.

Falcon and FalconGuide are registered trademarks of The Globe Pequot Press.

Library of Congress Cataloging-in-Publication Data
Regnier, Linda, 1944-
    Best easy day hikes, Santa Fe / by Linda and Katie Regnier.
        p.   cm.
    ISBN 1-56044-700-1 (pbk.)
    1. Hiking--New Mexico--Santa Fe Region Guidebooks.   2. Santa Fe
Region (N.M.) Guidebooks.   I. Regnier, Katie.   II. Title.
GV199.42.N62S277   1999
917.89'5604'53--dc21   99-29378

Manufactured in the United States of America
First Edition/Fourth Printing

CAUTION

Outdoor recreational activities are by their very nature potentially hazardous. All participants in such activities must assume responsibility for their own actions and safety. The information contained in this guidebook cannot replace sound judgment and good decision-making skills, which help reduce risk exposure, nor does the scope of this book allow for disclosure of all the potential hazards and risks involved in such activities.

Learn as much as possible about the outdoor recreational activities in which you participate, prepare for the unexpected, and be cautious. The reward will be a safer and more enjoyable experience.

Contents

Acknowledgments

This book would not have happened if not for our family. Thank you, Annie, for giving us the idea and motivation. Thanks to Krisi, Thalin, and Hope for providing us with a much needed break. Most of all, thank you, Jim, for supporting us throughout the entire process.

We would also like to thank many of our old and new friends, who helped out during our summer in Santa Fe. Richard Atkinson at the New Mexico Public Lands Information Center was always cheerful when we walked through his door with a new dilemma. His expertise was essential for the completion of this work. The park rangers at Hyde State Park were also friendly and helpful. We would like to thank Kristi Beguin at the DOME in Los Alamos for her personal guidance and Eloise Serna, who provided us with new energy and great conversation on several hikes. Thanks to the Serna and Aamodt families for their hospitality and showers!

Map Legend

Interstate		Picnic Area	
U.S. Highway		Campground	▲
State or County Road		Bridge	
Interstate Highway		Mine Site	✕
Paved Road		Cave	
Unpaved Road, Graded		Cabins/Buildings	■
Unpaved Road, Poor		Ruins	▫
Trailhead	○	Ranger Station	
Main Trail		Elevation	X 9,782 ft.
Secondary Trail		Butte	
Trailless Route		Cliffs	Top edge
Colorado River		Falls, Pouroff	
River/Creek, Perennial		Pass/Saddle	)(
Rapids		Gate	•——•
Drainage, Intermittent Creek		Sand Dunes	
Spring			
Forest/Wilderness/ Park Boundary			
State Boundary	ARIZONA UTAH		

Map Orientation

N

Scale

0   30   60

Miles

Overview Map

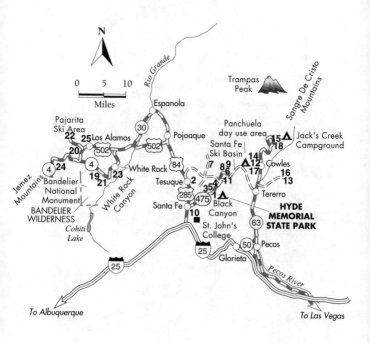

Ranking the Hikes

Introduction

Climb the mountains and get their glad tidings. Nature's
peace will flow into you as the sunshine flows into the trees.
The winds blow their freshness into you and the storms their
energy while cares drop away like the leaves of autumn.

—*John Muir*

Our goals in undertaking this project were both self-indul-
gent—to spend a summer in northern New Mexico hiking
together, mother and daughter—and altruistic—to share the
wilderness with you as completely as possible in a day-hike
fashion. Above all, it was our sincere desire that we in some
measure heighten awareness for the necessity to conserve
wilderness areas everywhere.

We have arranged 25 hikes according to three different
geographical areas, all within approximately an hour's drive
of Santa Fe. We give options ranging from high mountain
peaks to low-lying canyons. These are unique places, most
offering engrossing glimpses into the culture and history of
northern New Mexico, as well as a wilderness experience. We
urge you to read each hike carefully and to consider your physical ability, time restraints, and level of motivation in order to
choose wisely. Remember to keep in mind not only the length
of the hike but the elevation gain as well.

Much of our hiking was done in early June, and we found
ourselves trekking through and over snowdrifts in higher

elevations. These hikes are generally off limits in the winter. Lower elevation hikes may have year-round access, but may be icy; therefore, caution should be exercised, especially on steep slopes in winter.

Wildflowers are ever changing. Our observations may be entirely different from your experience. Expect the unexpected—wonderful discoveries await you on each hike.

Day hiking can be as satisfying as a long mountain excursion; however, preparation for any hike is time consuming, and day hikes are no exception. Once you "get it together" in your backpack, you are always ready to go. Essential items include topographical map, compass, first-aid kit, sunscreen, flashlight, insect repellent, matches, toilet paper and trowel, sunglasses, pocketknife, lip balm, layers of clothing ranging from warm to cool, rain gear, and food and water (never drink from mountain streams or lakes without purification). Other important items are a hat for intense summer sun, and extra socks and shoes for stream crossings. A personal favorite of ours was a large bandana hung on our backpack and used for everything from a handkerchief to a towel.

Careful consideration to the ethics of hiking is an essential ingredient to the preservation of wilderness. All hikers have the responsibility to know and follow the principles of "Leave No Trace." There are three rules: leave with everything you brought in, leave no sign of your visit, and leave the landscape as you found it. In the dry New Mexico terrain, it is difficult for anything to disintegrate; therefore, leave nothing behind—not even an orange peel! Also, be certain to cut down on erosion, another major issue in this environment, by staying on the trail at all times and resting on durable surfaces. Bury your waste 6 to 8 inches deep (packing out toilet paper) and at least 300 feet from a water source. Keep in mind that it is unlawful to remove archaeological artifacts (regardless of how tempting) or to disturb ruins. Even touching can be harmful to these priceless objects and locations.

Keep in mind several safety issues when hiking for any distance. It is our experience that hiking alone can be problematic, especially if you are hurt on the trail; however, this is definitely a personal issue and decision. Alone or not, be certain to inform someone of your destination and expected time of return. Before you set out, check weather conditions and plan accordingly. For example, it may be wise to plan an early day hike during northern New Mexico's rainy months of July and August. Severe midday lightning storms make high mountain passes and peaks perilous and make low-lying areas prone to flash flooding. Learn about the wildlife you may encounter while hiking, and never get too close. As you may have guessed, rattlesnakes definitely fall under this rule. Many varieties can be found in New Mexico, from desert areas to conifer forests; therefore, always be aware of where you are placing your hands, watch your step, stay on the trail, and carry a snakebite kit. A final word of caution involves the human animal. Do not leave valuables in your car, as trailheads are not patrolled. Although we have selected hikes originating in areas we considered more safe than others, there is no guarantee that your car will not be vandalized.

As with any exercise program, take care to monitor your own physical abilities. This calls to mind an extremely important health precaution before heading out on the trail: Allow time for your body to acclimate to the altitude of northern New Mexico. Tourists coming from low altitudes for a short visit to this area are particularly vulnerable to altitude sickness or acute mountain sickness (AMS). The city of Santa Fe is 7,000 feet above sea level, and many of the trailheads start at even higher elevations. AMS is the result of low air pressure at high elevations, causing low blood oxygen. Often healthy people, flying to Santa Fe from sea level, do not display symptoms of sickness until they reach between 8,000 and 10,000 feet in elevation. Signs of AMS include headache, loss of appetite, shortness of breath with exertion, insomnia, and lassitude. Moderate rest combined with light exercise and drinking plenty of water should relieve symptoms; however, if not, immediately descend 1,500 to 2,000 feet.

More serious are the conditions of high altitude cerebral edema (HACE) and high altitude pulmonary edema (HAPE). These are most likely to occur when several days are spent above 10,000 feet; however, they can occur in lower elevations. Symptoms of HACE are similar to those of AMS, in addition to unbearable headaches, vomiting, disorientation, hallucinations, and loss of coordination. Symptoms of HAPE include shortness of breath and a crackling sound in the chest. Both conditions are life-threatening and demand an immediate descent to lower elevations and medical attention.

Do not let this litany of preparations and precautions frighten you. After careful planning, your mind will be eased and your hiking experience matchless.

Santa Fe

Santa Fe represents a unique blend of the Spanish, Mexican, American Indian, and North American cultures, which permeates every aspect of life and activity in northern New Mexico. For happenings in Santa Fe and vicinity consult the book *Insider's Guide to Santa Fe*.

With the exception of one hike originating in the picturesque village of Tesuque, the hikes closest to Santa Fe begin and end in the Sangre de Cristo Mountains. Named the "blood of Christ" because of their color at sunset, these mountains have the highest elevation of any range in New Mexico. Because of their proximity to Santa Fe, these hikes are frequently busier after work hours when people wish to get some quick exercise, and on weekends. The trails are well worn and well maintained and service not only hikers but hikers and their dogs, runners, and mountain bikers.

There are numerous campgrounds north of Santa Fe on New Mexico Highway 475. Black Canyon, a USDA Forest Service campground, is located in a heavily wooded and shaded area and has excellent facilities, including a campground host and the availability of reservations. Hyde Memorial State Park is only 8 miles from Santa Fe and is the highest state park in New Mexico at 8,500 feet. This 350-acre park has 75 camping sites, 7 of which are designated RV, with water and electricity. Most of the tent sites have shelters, toilets, and water nearby, and we also spotted a centrally located new playground. Big Tesuque and Aspen Vista are farther up NM 475, closer to Santa Fe Ski Basin, and accommodate tent camping.

1
BLACK CANYON TRAIL

Type of hike: Loop.
Distance: 2 miles, round trip.
Elevaton gain: 450 feet.
Maps: McClure Reservoir (USGS).

Finding the trailhead: From Santa Fe Plaza drive north on Washington Avenue. At the first light after the intersection with Paseo de Peralta, turn right onto Artist's Road, which becomes New Mexico Highway 475. At approximately 7 miles turn right (east) into Black Canyon Campground. Parking is allocated for hikers outside the campground entrance. Walk uphill through the campground to campsite number 4, where you will find a trailhead sign.

The hike: This hike, close to Santa Fe, is suitable for children. It is easy, well shaded, and a good introduction to mountain terrain, fir-aspen belt vegetation, and wildflowers. In early summer we found red columbine, clematis, false solomon's seal, and oregon grape.

The first section of the hike is a gradual ascent on a wide, somewhat rocky path. At about 0.5 mile there is a fork in the trail and a wooden sign displaying a double arrow. Proceed left (southeast) for the Black Canyon Loop. The trail immediately veers to the right (southwest) and begins an uphill climb. At 0.8 mile you will reach another fork, an unmarked

Black Canyon Trail

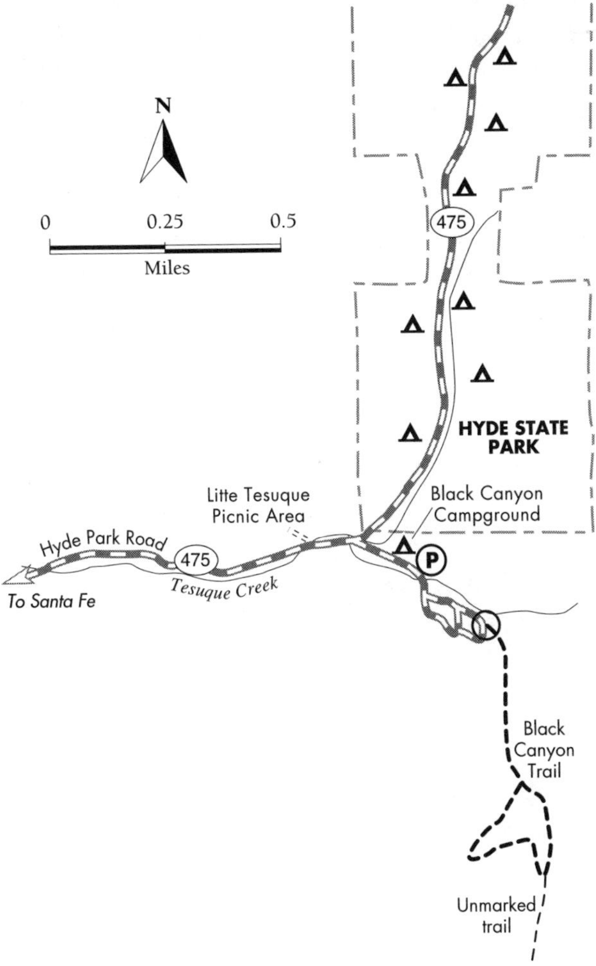

N

| 0 | 0.25 | 0.5 |

Miles

475

Litte Tesuque
Picnic Area

Hyde Park Road 475

Tesuque Creek

To Santa Fe

HYDE STATE
PARK

Black Canyon
Campground

P

Black
Canyon
Trail

Unmarked
trail

trail. Follow this trail to the right (north). Almost immediately a sign reading "Stay on Trail" appears. Although this warning is posted for hikers making this loop in reverse, it is important information. The watershed for Santa Fe (to your left, south, over the saddle) is out of bounds for hikers, and a heavy fine is imposed for trespassing. Stay right of the sign, following the descending unmarked trail. You will walk through a beautiful aspen grove on your way to the intersection with the original route. Retrace your steps and finish up your hike at Black Canyon Campground campsite number 4.

2
TESUQUE CREEK

Type of hike: Loop.
Distance: 3 miles, round trip.
Elevaton gain: 400 feet.
Maps: Santa Fe (USGS).

Finding the trailhead: From Santa Fe Plaza drive north on Washington Avenue (which will become Bishop's Lodge Road), for 4.5 miles. At this point the main road takes a turn to the left. Do not follow the main road but take a sharp right to Big Tesuque Canyon, a dirt road, where you will quickly come to a small area designated as trail parking. A second parking lot is a short distance up the road. Walk along this road until you come to several wooden posts on the right (south) side, indicating the beginning of the trail.

The hike: It is a quick drive from Santa Fe to picturesque Tesuque. This easy hike offers exposure to lower-elevation vegetation, including pinyon-juniper and oak-pine belts. The creek is easily accessed; its water provides welcome relief on hot summer days.

Almost immediately after passing through the wooden posts, you will cross Big Tesuque Creek on a permanent bridge. Follow the trail upstream, beside the fenced-in back-yards of a unique residential district, until you reach an intersection with a private drive. Turn left (north), cross the

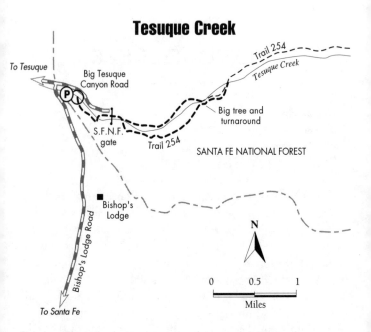

Tesuque Creek

To Tesuque

Big Tesuque
Canyon Road

P

S.F.N.F.
gate

Trail 254

Trail 254

Tesuque Creek

Big tree and
turnaround

SANTA FE NATIONAL FOREST

Bishop's
Lodge

Bishop's Lodge Road

To Santa Fe

N

0   0.5   1
Miles

car bridge, and follow Winsor Trail 254 to the right (east).
In about half a mile you will pass through a gate, indicating
an entrance to the Santa Fe National Forest. Make sure that
you take the right fork of the trail. The left fork is the loop
on which you will return.

The goal now is to get to the opposite side of the creek.
This can be a daunting task in spring and early summer
runoff, so an extra pair of shoes might be in order. Do not
take the first crossing, which has a steep slope on the opposite side of the creek. Look for a second crossing, where
there is an obvious trail ascending the hillside across the

creek. Follow this trail, traversing the side of the ridge. Soon you will cross a dry arroyo and the trail will split (there are no trail signs). Take the main trail to the right (south), climbing an extremely rocky hill. Near the top is a junction. Take Winsor Trail 254 to the left(north) and follow it as it parallels the stream below.

A large ponderosa pine (about 2 feet in diameter) to your left (north) marks the return trail. If you come to another stream crossing you have gone too far and need to turn back, locating the large ponderosa, which will now be on your right. The trail downhill, past the ponderosa, takes you to a fallen log, which provides sturdy passage to the north side of the stream. The trail now ascends and descends as it heads back down the canyon. Summer months can be especially hot and dry on this slope, as evidenced by the presence of cholla and prickly pear cacti. Loop back to the original trail near the first stream crossing and retrace your route back to the trailhead and your car.

3
CHAMISA TRAIL

Type of hike: Out-and-back.
Distance: 4.8 miles, round trip.
Elevaton gain: 700 feet.
Maps: Aspen Basin and McClure Reservoir (USGS), Pecos Wilderness (USFS).

Finding the trailhead: From Santa Fe Plaza drive north on Washington Avenue. Proceed through the intersection with Paseo de Peralta and turn right at the first light onto Artist's Road, which becomes New Mexico Highway 475. At 5.6 miles there is a large parking area on the left (north). The trailhead is located at the east end of the parking lot.

The hike: This hike is close to Santa Fe and offers a good workout as well as great exposure to pinyon-juniper and mixed-conifer vegetation belts. The reward for the uphill exertion is a welcome descent into the Big Tesuque Creek basin where you can rest amid cool water, wildflowers, and a green meadow. Mountain bikers, runners, and dogs frequent this trail, especially after work and on weekends.

The trailhead is marked with a signpost and quickly turns north along the canyon. This gradual climb is sunny, warm, and dry in summer, and it may be a good idea to wait for a late-afternoon starting time. You may also want to grab a hat to ward off the heat. After a 700-foot ascent, 1.3 miles

Chamisa Trail

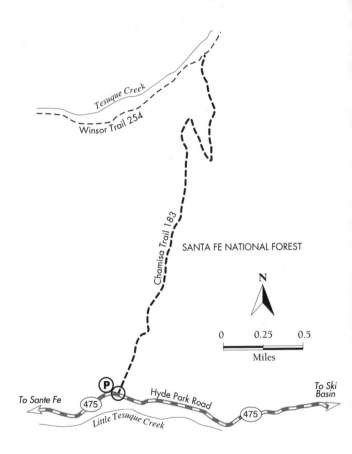

from the trailhead, you will come to the top of a ridge. You may notice another trail coming in from the canyon below. This is an alternate route from the parking lot where you began your hike. Turn right (southeast) and follow the main trail downhill, descending into a canyon where the trail parallels a small stream. This portion of the hike is cool and shaded, and wildflowers thrive in early summer.

At 2.3 miles are two trail markers on wooden posts, indicating an intersection with Winsor Trail 254. This ends the Chamisa Trail, but be aware that to the immediate right is a pristine meadow providing pleasant resting places near the creek or on a large granite boulder. Take note of the field of wild flag (Rocky Mountain iris) in early summer. Also keep an eye out for the colorful western tanager and the Steller's jay who frequent the meadowlands.

Retrace your steps for your return hike, turning left (south) at the two posted signs near the meadow. When you reach the saddle be certain to go left (south) on the middle trail to return to the parking lot.

4
BORREGO–BEAR WALLOW–
WINSOR TRIANGLE

Type of hike: Loop.
Distance: 4 miles, round trip.
Elevaton gain: 770 feet.
Maps: Aspen Basin and McClure Reservoir (USGS), Pecos
Wilderness (USFS).

Finding the trailhead: From Santa Fe Plaza drive north on
Washington Avenue. Proceed through the intersection with
Paseo de Peralta and turn right at the first light onto Artist's
Road, which becomes New Mexico Highway 475. Drive
8.5 miles to a parking lot on the left side of the road. Hyde
Park RV Campground is on the left (west) about a quarter-
mile from this turn, so be alert.

The hike: This hike, which uses Borrego Trail (150), Bear
Wallow Trail (182), and Winsor Trail (254), is wonderfully
close to Santa Fe and a quick way to get the flavor of the
mountains and streams of the Sangre de Cristos. It is popular with runners, dogs, and bikers, so be prepared for all
kinds of company, especially on weekends.

The trailhead is located at the far end of the parking lot.
The sign reads, "Borrego Trail 150, 1.5 miles to Trail 254."
White fir, Douglas-fir, Rocky Mountain maple, and large
aspen line this wide, well-worn trail, which was once used

Borrego–Bear Wallow–Winsor Triangle

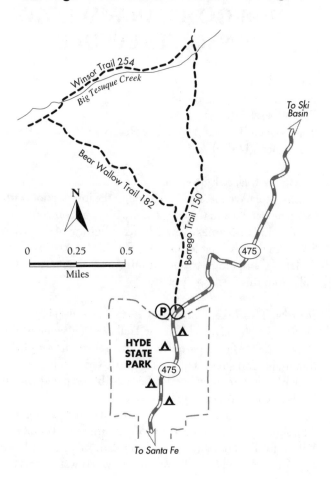

to herd sheep to market from the north. After an easy 0.5 mile, turn left (northwest) at the junction of Borrego Trail 150 and Bear Wallow Trail 182. On your return you will loop back to this point on Borrego Trail. For the next mile you will follow Bear Wallow to the crossing of Big Tesuque Creek. Watch for changes in vegetation, especially on the southern slope, before you reach the stream crossing. We felt fortunate to find a tufted evening primrose just before starting the switchbacks leading to the creek. Several logs provide a safe crossing, and you will immediately come to the junction of Bear Wallow 182 and Winsor Trail 254. This is a great place to rest; look for wild raspberries late in summer, and prepare for the uphill trek on your return. Take a right (east) onto Winsor Trail 254. Notice the charming miniature waterfalls as you parallel the creek and walk steadily uphill.

At 2.5 miles you will encounter Borrego Trail 150 once again. Take a right (south) to begin the last leg of your hike. It takes but a minute and you once again cross a creek. A large, fallen ponderosa pine provides a bridge, and it has created a great swimming spot, beckoning you to take another break from the heat before the climb ahead. The trail ascends on switchbacks then descends, and at 3.5 miles you will pass the Bear Wallow junction, which was your original route to the Big Tesuque Creek. Continue straight ahead on Borrego Trail, retracing your steps back to the trailhead.

5
HYDE MEMORIAL PARK LOOP

Type of hike: Loop.
Distance: 4 miles, round trip.
Elevaton gain: 1,000 feet.
Maps: Hyde Memorial State Park brochure available from New Mexico State Parks Division (see For More Information).

Finding the trailhead: From the Santa Fe Plaza drive north on Washington Avenue. Proceed through the intersection with Paseo de Peralta and turn right at the first light onto Artist's Road, which becomes New Mexico Highway 475. Drive approximately 7.4 miles until you reach the Hyde Memorial State Park Headquarters on the right (east). Park here and cross the street (west) to the trailhead.

The hike: This hike is relatively short and, while not altogether easy because of some steep elevation gain, is well worth the effort for its panoramic mountain and valley views.

Take the stone bridge over Little Tesuque Creek, and head left (south) up a rather steep set of switchbacks. We saw many small reptiles on this dry slope. The first section of this hike can be strenuous and hot in the summer; be sure to take an adequate supply of water.

After climbing 1,000 feet you will reach the top of the ridge. Because of extraordinary weather conditions there are

Hyde Memorial Park Loop

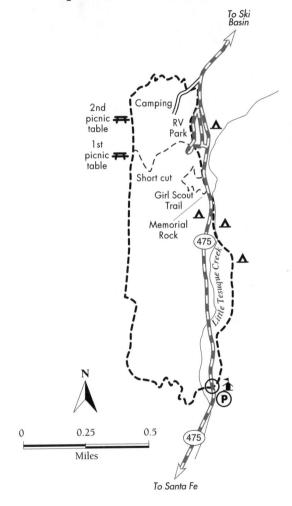

a great number of fallen trees in this area. Rather quickly you will come upon the first of two picnic tables. Just beyond the table, to your right (east), is a trail that switchbacks down to the Hyde Park RV Campground and the main highway. However, it is very difficult to locate because of the downed trees, and we recommend remaining on the main trail and hiking to the second picnic table. From this ridge you can spot the Sandia Mountains to the southwest, and to the northwest, across the Rio Grande valley, the Jemez Mountain range. About 0.1 mile farther along the ridge the trail turns right and descends on a series of switchbacks, ending in a small campground just north of the RV park. Rather than walking back on the highway (NM 475), we suggest that you take any one of the trails that parallel it, heading downhill (south) toward park headquarters. You may run into the Girl Scout Trail with its rock borders and identified and labeled trees and plants, although many seem to have disappeared over the years. When you reach a large memorial rock adjacent to the highway, cross the road and follow Little Tesuque Creek back to the parking lot and your car.

6
LA VEGA

Type of hike: Out-and-back.
Distance: 6.5 miles, round trip.
Elevaton gain: 1,500 feet.
Maps: Aspen Basin (USGS), Pecos Wilderness (SFNF).

Finding the trailhead: From Santa Fe Plaza drive north on Washington Avenue. Turn right at the first light after the intersection with Paseo de Peralta onto Artist's Road, which becomes New Mexico Highway 475 and ends 14 miles from this point, at the ski basin. Park in the lower lot and walk north, toward Tesuque Creek, where you will see a large signpost for the Pecos Wilderness and also a marker for Winsor Trail 254.

The hike: Because this trail begins at the Santa Fe Ski Basin, it has less use than those closer to Santa Fe. Its destination is a beautiful valley complete with a stream running through it and a close view of Santa Fe Baldy. The maps of the area do not give the complete details of this hike; however, the trail is indicated by a trail marker and is easy to find.

Begin by crossing the bridge over Tesuque Creek and following Winsor Trail 254 to the right (east). In early summer marsh marigolds line the creek. As you ascend on switchbacks for the next 0.5 mile, aspen and mixed conifer forests and meadows enclose you. The gate, indicating entrance to the

21

La Vega

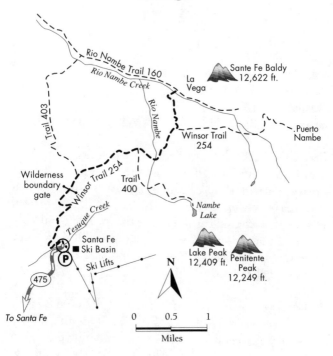

Pecos Wilderness, is a welcome sight, as the only ascent for this hike is now over! If you stop to rest you may be visited by some resident gray jays looking for a handout.

The trail now descends for about a mile. You will pass a trail marker for Rio Nambe Trail 403 and another for Nambe Lake Trail 400; however, stay on Winsor Trail as it crosses Nambe Creek and continues north. After about 2 miles you will see a sign on the right side of the trail for Upper Nambe Trail 101, Rio Nambe, and La Vega. Turn left (northeast) and start your descent into a beautiful grassy meadow with a large aspen stand.

You now descend to the lowest part of the hike, and cross Rio Nambe Creek on logs (take care in wet weather). Head left (west), uphill, and come to the junction with Rio Nambe Trail 160 (about 3 miles into the hike). Go left (west) on Trail 160, which is rocky and narrow at this point. After a gradual descent and another ascent, you will find you have moved away from the creek and are very soon in a clearing. The sign indicating you have reached La Vega may or may not be still standing, as vandals often consider these signs a treasure; however, if you walk a few yards ahead, you will find yourself at your destination—a vast meadow at the foot of Santa Fe Baldy. Enjoy exploring and resting. Begin your return trip at the signpost, following Trail 160 back to the creek and then retracing your steps back to trail 254, where you will turn right (west) to return to Santa Fe Ski Basin.

7
RIO NAMBE CREEK

Type of hike: Out-and-back.
Distance: 4.5 miles, round trip.
Elevaton gain: 1,000 feet.
Maps: Aspen Basin (USGS), Pecos Wilderness (USFS).

Finding the trailhead: From Santa Fe Plaza drive north on Washington Avenue. Drive through the intersection with Paseo de Peralta and turn right at the first light, onto Artist's Road, which becomes New Mexico Highway 475. From this turn drive a little more than 12 miles to Forest Road 102, on your left (west). After turning onto this dirt road, drive approximately 3 miles until you reach an intersection with FR 412. Here you will drive right (north) on FR 412 for approximately 1.4 miles, coming to a parking lot on the right, next to a trailhead entrance. Park your car here but do not use this trail. Walk a short distance farther up the road to the north and take Trails 163 and 150 to the left (west). The continuation of this road leads to Aspen Ranch; however it belongs to Tesuque Pueblo and is closed to public use.

The hike: This hike, which uses Borrego Trail 150, is varied in terrain. A long portion of it parallels a lush streambed, making it a great choice for a hot summer day. Although this trail is accessible and within easy driving distance from Santa Fe, it appeared more isolated than other trails in the ski basin

Rio Nambe Creek

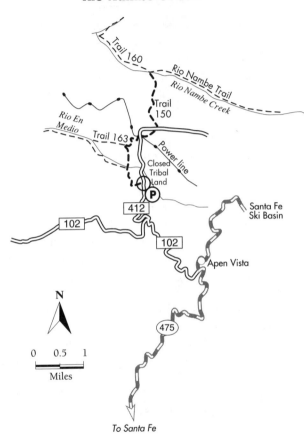

area; we met no other people on a midweek hike in mid-June.

You will ascend as you begin the hike, but soon will start a gentle descent through a series of switchbacks in a mixed conifer and aspen forest. You may run into some very verbal cattle grazing on and around this part of the trail; however, they have no interest in accompanying you, so just walk casually through them. At the bottom of this canyon, you will cross the Rio en Medio.

Continue following the trail uphill; a trail marker points out that you are, indeed, still on Borrego Trail 150. At this point Trail 163 cuts off to the west, but continue straight ahead (north). Ascend to the top of the ridge through a series of switchbacks. Here the trail intersects with the original dirt road. A trail marker marks Borrego Trail and Rancho Viejo to the left (west). Follow the road uphill through aspen groves and meadows, and you will pass under a set of powerlines. At the top of the next rise is a trail marker for Borrego Trail 150, Rio Nambe, and Rancho Viejo.

Take Trail 150 to the left (northwest), descending until you reach the canyon floor. It is an easy hike along this lush drainage to Rio Nambe Creek. If you wish to extend your hike a short distance, cross the log bridge, and immediately Trail 150 merges with Rio Nambe Trail 160. Follow the trail upstream (east) to a large open meadow, rest awhile, and then return, retracing your steps back to the trailhead.

8
PUERTO NAMBE MEADOW

Type of hike: Out-and-back.
Distance: 8 miles, round trip.
Elevaton gain: 1,150 feet.
Maps: Aspen Basin (USGS), Pecos Wilderness (USFS).

Finding the trailhead: From Santa Fe Plaza drive north on Washington Avenue. At the first light after the intersection with Paseo de Peralta turn right onto Artist's Road, which becomes New Mexico Highway 475 and ends approximately 14 miles from this point, at the Santa Fe Ski Basin. Park in the lower lot and walk north, toward the creek, where you will see a large signpost for the Pecos Wilderness and a marker for Winsor Trail 254.

The hike: This hike, along Winsor Trail 254, is well worth the time and energy necessary in order to obtain spectacular views of the peaks and valleys surrounding Santa Fe.

Begin by crossing the bridge at the marker for Winsor Trail 254 and turning right (east). In early summer white and yellow marsh marigolds line the creek. As you ascend on switchbacks for the next 0.5 mile, lovely aspen and mixed conifer forests and gentle meadows surround you. The fence and gate, designating entrance to the Pecos Wilderness, are welcome sights, as this first ascent is now over! If you stop to rest you may be visited by some resident gray jays looking for a handout.

Puerto Nambe Meadow

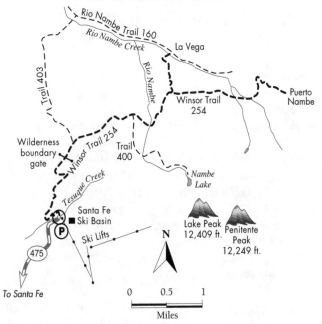

The trail now descends for about a mile. You will pass a marker for Rio Nambe Trail 403 and another for Nambe Lake Trail; however, stay on Winsor Trail as it crosses Nambe Creek and continues north. A little over 2 miles into the hike you will see a sign on the right side of the trail, pointing left, for Upper Nambe Trail 101, Rio Nambe, and La Vega. You are now approximately 1.5 miles from Puerto Nambe. Continue straight ahead on Winsor Trail as it passes through a small grassy meadow. When you are once again in the conifer forest a trail marker indicates Rio Nambe Trail 160 to your left. Remain on Winsor Trail. During late spring and early summer this trail seems to double as a small stream. It is a short hike through water and mud until you come to a set of challenging switchbacks, which leads you to the beautiful meadows and views of Puerto Nambe. As you walk into the meadow incredible vistas await you of Penitente Peak to the south, Lake Peak to the southwest and Santa Fe Baldy to the north. The distant valley views are equal in grandeur. As you walk through the meadow look for a trail marker that signifies the junction of Skyline and Winsor trails and points the way to Lake Katherine (north). You might want to rest here and plan future hikes.

The trip home is quite painless—a reward for the uphill switchbacks you endured. Follow Winsor Trail back to the ski basin.

9
RAVEN'S RIDGE

Type of hike: Out-and-back.
Distance: 6 miles, round trip.
Elevaton gain: 1,600 feet.
Maps: Aspen Basin (USGS) (complete trail not marked),
Pecos Wilderness (USFS) (complete trail not marked).

Finding the trailhead: From Santa Fe Plaza drive north on
Washington Avenue. At the first light after the intersection
with Paseo de Peralta, turn right onto Artist's Road, which
becomes New Mexico Highway 475 and ends approximately
14 miles from this point at the Santa Fe Ski Basin. Park in
the lower lot and walk north, toward Tesuque Creek, where
you will see a large signpost for the Pecos Wilderness and a
marker for Winsor Trail 254.

The hike: Although this hike is not on the topo map or in
other hiking books, it is easy to find, as much of it parallels
the Pecos Wilderness boundary. The gain in elevation looks
impressive; however, this did not feel like a strenuous ascent.
It is frequented by a number of hikers, even on weekdays.

Begin by crossing the bridge at the marker for Winsor
Trail 254 and turning right (east). In early summer yellow
and white marsh marigolds line the creek. As you ascend on
switchbacks for the next 0.5 mile, aspen and mixed conifer
forests as well as gentle meadows surround you. At 0.5 mile

you will reach the fence and gate signifying the entrance into the Pecos Wilderness. You may want to stop and rest awhile because another gain in elevation awaits you. Do not go through the gate but walk right (east) on the trail that parallels the wooden fence.

Your gradual ascent through aspen and Engelmann spruce forest is on a narrow and rocky, but easy to locate, trail. As the elevation gains, notice the change in vegetation. At 11,380 feet, or about 1.5 miles from the trailhead, you will come to a granite outcrop, affording a wonderful view of Santa Fe Baldy straight ahead of you (northeast) and Lake Peak to your right (southeast). You can also see the pristine green meadow of La Vega. Your destination, the granite outcrop in the foreground as you look to the right or east of Lake Peak, is clearly visible.

The next segment of this hike is uphill and somewhat rigorous; therefore, if you are looking for a more moderate hike, this is a good turn-around point. If you continue, the trail steadily ascends to your right (southeast). Soon you will come to an area of large granite boulders on the west side of the ridge. Before you is a view of the entire valley from the Jemez Mountains (west) to the Sandia Mountains (south). Continue uphill (southeast) to another group of large boulders. In mid-July beautiful clumps of wild blue columbine were growing in this area. The trail skirts the boulders on the left side, and within a short distance you will reach the top of the ridge and a small meadow.

The remainder of the hike is relatively easy, with gentle ups and downs and impressive vistas on both sides of the ridge. As you ascend the last hill before reaching your destination,

Raven's Ridge

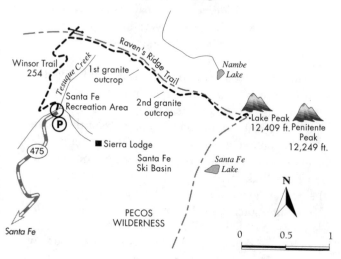

you may want to walk to the edge of the cliff on the left (north) side of the trail for a view of Nambe Lake far below. One final push brings you to the end of your hike at a large granite outcropping, which gives you an "up close and personal" view of Lake Peak to the east. The elevation is 12,000 feet, and you will notice from your resting place there are descents in every direction. To return, retrace your steps; however, if you find yourself on a different route do not be concerned—all the trails eventually converge, and you can easily find the fence boundary. Follow it, retracing your steps to the wilderness gate, and then descend the switchbacks on Trail 254 to the parking lot.

10
ATALAYA MOUNTAIN

Type of hike: Out-and-back.
Distance: 7 miles round trip from St. John's College; approximately 4.6 miles round trip from Ponderosa Ridge residential community.
Elevaton gain: From St. John's College parking lot: 1,781 feet; from Ponderosa Ridge residential area: 1,661 feet.
Maps: Santa Fe (USGS).

Finding the trailhead: From downtown Santa Fe take Alameda Avenue east (paralleling the Santa Fe River). Turn right (south) on Camino Cabra and continue until it intersects with Camino de Cruz Blanca. Turn left (west) at this intersection, and you will see St. John's College on your immediate right (south) along with a sign that indicates parking for the Atalaya Mountain Trailhead. Here you have two options: a hike of 7 miles from the far (east) end of this parking lot on Trail 174 or a shorter hike of about 4.6 miles on Trail 170 (which eventually joins Trail 174). To reach this trailhead drive 0.8 mile beyond St. John's College on Camino de Cruz Blanca to a small parking lot on the left side of the road. Ponderosa Ridge residential development begins at this point, and there is a large, informative marker here for Trail 170.

The hike: This hike begins on the outskirts of the city of Santa Fe and affords panoramic views of the Rio Grande valley and the city of Santa Fe as well as an introduction to the vegetation characteristic of the foothills and mountains of this area.

There is an optional trailhead, beginning in a residential district, which deletes the first portion of the hike in the area surrounding St. John's College.

This can be a hot hike in summer, so a late afternoon starting time is advisable. Be sure to carry enough water. Also, be aware that this trail passes through private land (from trailhead to national forest boundary); therefore, please stay on the trails.

Option 1. As you stand in the parking lot you can spot Atalaya Mountain with its granite ridges to the east. The first section of Trail 174 is surrounded by chamisa shrubs, prickly pear cactus, juniper, and pinyon. If it is early summer look for beautiful pink New Mexican locust, blooming Apache plume, lupine, and phlox. Soon you will walk through one large, dry arroyo with a sign keeping you on Trail 174. A second arroyo and a small wooden gate follow. About a mile into the hike, cross a dirt road and head up wooden steps. Here at 7,630 feet the vegetation changes to ponderosa pine and mixed conifers.

At approximately 1.5 miles a perplexing trail sign indicates Trail 17 (it should read Trail 170). Atalaya Mountain is 2 miles from here. Walk through the gate and head right (east). As you walk the switchbacks notice a great view of the Jemez Mountains to the west. Soon a marker shows Atalaya straight ahead, and shortly after that a marker presents you with the choice of a steep or easy route to the summit. We chose the easy trail, which did not prove to be

Atalaya Mountain

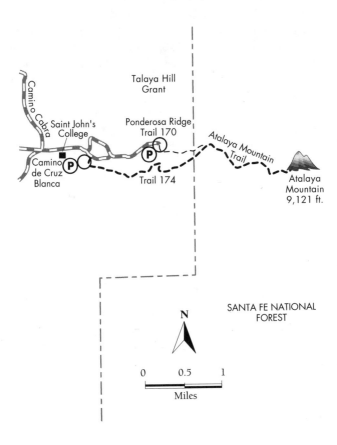

all that easy. Follow the well-worn main trail, often marked by blue metal diamonds tacked onto trees.

At an elevation of 8,270 feet a flat area provides a good resting point or perhaps a turnaround point. The hike beyond this point is strenuous, yet has some wonderful valley views. If you continue, a series of switchbacks awaits you. Douglas fir lines the trail, and at the top of the ridge, near the summit are unusual quartz and lichen formations. Follow the trail to the highest point and enjoy the view and your accomplishment. You might also keep your eyes out for black-capped chickadees and woodpeckers. Retrace your steps—downhill!

Option 2: The trail marker for Trail 170 is located in the parking area and indicates that Atalaya Mountain summit is 2.3 miles from this point, with an elevation gain of 1,661 feet. Begin by following the trail (south) along the wall of the residential development for a short distance to a gate on your left. Enter through the gate on the pedestrian walk, still following Trail 170, and continue uphill on the road until you reach the top. You will see wooden steps in front of you leading to a fenced area (the road continues off to the right). Walk through the gate; another trail marker appears for Trail 170. Proceed uphill to the junction with Trail 174.

11
TESUQUE PEAK

Type of hike: Out-and-Back.
Distance: 12 miles, round trip.
Elevaton gain: 1,970 feet.
Maps: Aspen Basin (USGS), Pecos Wilderness (USFS).

Finding the trailhead: From Santa Fe Plaza drive north on Washington Avenue. Drive through the intersection with Paseo de Peralta and turn right at the first light onto Artist's Road, which becomes New Mexico Highway 475. Go 13 miles to Aspen Vista, which is on the right side of the road. The trail starts after the gate at the upper (north) end of the parking lot.

The hike: This hike, which begins at Aspen Vista Campground, is considered moderate in spite of the distance it covers. It follows Forest Road 150 with no steep inclines out-and-back. We found that the wide, fairly even road makes it possible to hike side-by-side, which is a nice change from most mountain trails. Because of the elevation the weather can be unpredictable, so take along layers for every kind of weather. The high-elevation views afforded on this trail are spectacular, and it is therefore a very popular hike.

After walking through the Aspen Vista Campground gate, you will be instantly surrounded by aspen forest, mak-

Tesuque Peak

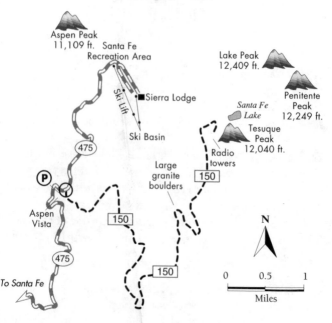

ing this an ideal fall hike; however, when we hiked in early summer wildflowers were abundant. Although there are three stream crossings over tributaries of Tesuque Creek they are all covered by the road, so you need not worry about wet feet on this long hike. At about 1.5 miles a look across the valley offers excellent long-distance views of Los Alamos and Black Mesa (a sacred site adjacent to San Ildefonso Pueblo).

Notice the vegetation change as you climb. The aspen forest gives way to subalpine evergreens and Engelmann spruce. About 2.5 miles into the hike a series of switchbacks begins. We ran into some small snowfields in early June and started adding clothing to keep warm. At about 3.8 miles is a clearing with a spectacular panoramic view of the valley. Walk a bit longer and you will find the perfect picnic spot amidst large granite boulders. From this point you can see your destination near the microwave towers of Tesuque Peak. The snowfields we encountered made the trek to the top more difficult than it appeared from this point.

When you reach the summit, you may simply turn around and retrace your steps back to the car, or if you wish a speedier descent, you can choose a ski run. If you choose the latter, head northwest down the slope to the right of the first snowfence. Use the green metal roof below as your guide to the bottom of the hill and the parking lot. This descent will take approximately one hour. From the parking lot we decided to hitchhike the mile plus back to our car at Aspen Vista; however, during the week the cars were few and far between; consequently, we had to walk almost a mile before the one car we saw offered us a ride.

Pecos Wilderness

This 222,673-acre wilderness, most of which is located within the Santa Fe National Forest, lies 35 miles northeast of Santa Fe. Take Interstate 25 east from Santa Fe to the Glorieta exit and follow signs to the small town of Pecos. Here you may wish to make a side trip to the Pecos National Historical Park, where the ruins depict a thousand-year history of pueblo and Spanish mission life. From Pecos take New Mexico Highway 63 north to the Pecos Wilderness. Within the boundaries of the wilderness lie many peaks over 13,000 feet, mountain lakes, and more than 150 miles of pristine streams. This area is heavily used by hikers and horses; therefore, consider getting out early on weekends, especially if you are planning to locate a campsite in one of the many highly accessible and well-maintained campgrounds.

12
CAVE CREEK TRAIL

Type of hike: Out-and-back.
Distance: 8 miles, round trip.
Elevaton gain: 1,400 feet.
Maps: Cowles (USGS), Pecos Wilderness (USFS).

Finding the trailhead: From Santa Fe take U.S. Highway 25 toward Las Vegas. Take Exit 299 for New Mexico Highway 50, Glorieta and Pecos. Follow NM 50 to the town of Pecos and the intersection with NM 63. Turn left onto NM 63 and drive 20 miles to Cowles. In Cowles turn left over the bridge crossing the Pecos River, then turn at the first right onto the single-lane, paved Forest Road 305 to Panchuela Day Use Area. Park in the upper lot, as the lower lot is closed and has been blocked by large boulders. Walk through the boulders (north) to the lower lot and over the footbridge crossing Panchuela Creek. Cave Creek Trail begins here.

The hike: This hike takes you to an intersection with Trail 251. A set of caves along picturesque Cave Creek is its unique feature. It is appropriate as a family hike, especially if the caves are the turn-around point. This trail receives heavy use by hikers and horses. It will be a fee area in 1999, but at the publication of this book the fee was unestablished.

After crossing the creek head upstream to the left (northwest). The large, old Douglas-firs along the trail are im-

Cave Creek Trail

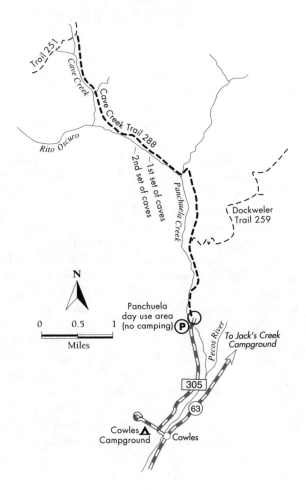

pressive, as are the wildflowers such as wild iris, bluebell, wild geranium, and shooting star, seen in early summer. As you hike, the trail parallels the creek, rises above it, and at about 0.8 mile comes to a junction with Dockweiler Trail 259, which forks to the right. Stay left (west) on Cave Creek 288 as it winds through the valley. We met several people hiking out after a successful day of fishing for brown trout.

At about 1.5 miles you will reach the confluence of Panchuela and Cave Creeks. Follow the trail to the left (west) over several logs, which make a rather precarious bridge. This is a beautiful spot to stop, rest, and examine the lush riparian vegetation.

The first set of caves lies a short distance up the trail on your left (south) and can be located by looking for a camping area nearby. They are more difficult to find than the larger, second set of caves—also marked by a camping spot and a fire pit—just a short distance up the trail. You can cross the creek to examine the caves; however, the rocks are very slippery, and there are deep drop-offs inside the caves, so it is not safe to enter them.

After exploring the caves, turn left (west) back onto Cave Creek Trail and begin a gradual ascent through alternating aspen meadows and lush creekside vegetation. The trail becomes steeper, and when you have climbed approximately 1,000 feet from Cave Creek you will reach a junction with Trail 251, which comes from the south and continues north to Horsethief Meadows. Large boulders beside the creek provide a cool resting place before you turn around and start the trip back to the trailhead.

13
MORA FLATS

Type of hike: Out-and-back.
Distance: 7 miles, round trip.
Elevaton gain: 400 feet.
Maps: Elk Mountain (USGS), Pecos Wilderness (USFS).

Finding the trailhead: From Santa Fe take U.S. Highway 25 toward Las Vegas. Take Exit 299 to New Mexico Highway 50, Glorieta, and Pecos. Follow NM 50 to the town of Pecos and the intersection with NM 63. Turn left onto NM 63 and drive to the small town of Terrero, which consists of a small grocery store-post office combination and a few homes. Drive approximately 5 miles beyond Terrero and turn right (east) at the sign for Iron Gate Campground. The dirt road to the campground, which is about 4 miles long, is often steep and has deep ditches; therefore, we recommend using a high-clearance vehicle and driving this trailhead during dry season because rain or snow would only intensify an already troublesome situation.

The trailhead for Hamilton Mesa 249, used for the first segment of this hike, is located at the far (northeast) end of the campground. There are parking spaces allotted for day hikers and backpacking hikers near the trailhead.

The hike: This is a pleasant hike, without extreme inclines. The trail winds through spruce, fir, and aspen forest to the

Mora Flats

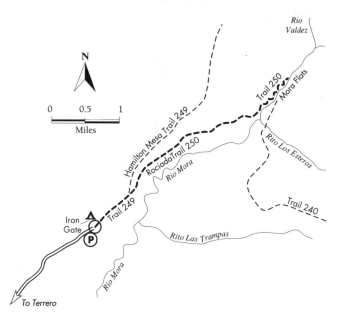

meadows of the Mora River. Early summer wildflowers are abundant. This will be a fee area in 1999, but at the publication of this book the fee was undetermined.

To begin this hike leave the campground through the iron gate; the well-worn trail heads east and gently climbs to the ridge above the Mora River. It doesn't take long to discover that this is also a trail well used by horses. At the top of the ridge there are several smaller trails leading to views of the Rio Mora Canyon to the right (east); however, to continue go left (north) along the the ridge until you reach a trail junction (about 1 mile from trailhead) of Hamilton Mesa Trail 249 heading to the left (northwest) and Rociada Trail 250 going to the right (northeast). Follow Trail 250 as it slowly descends past big old ponderosa pines, Douglas-firs, and aspen groves. Before reaching the flats you will go through a gate and fence and hike past an excellent spot for viewing Rio Mora far below the trail. Continue down a long segment of switchbacks to the river and enjoy a rest among the willows and wild iris. Mora Flats is a juncture for many trails servicing the Pecos Wilderness. It is also a good place to call it a day and turn around, retracing your steps back to the trailhead.

14
DOCKWEILER TRAIL

Type of hike: Out-and-back.
Distance: 6 miles, round trip.
Elevaton gain: 1,550 feet.
Maps: Cowles.

Finding the trailhead: From Santa Fe take U.S. Highway 25 toward Las Vegas. Take Exit 299 to New Mexico Highway 50, Glorieta, and Pecos. Follow NM 50 to the town of Pecos and the intersection with NM 63. Turn left onto NM 63 and drive 20 miles to Cowles, where you take a left over the bridge crossing the Pecos River. Take the first right on the single-lane, paved Forest Road 305 to Panchuela Day Use Area. Park in the upper lot, as the lower lot has been closed and is blocked by large boulders. Walk north through the boulders to the lower lot and over the footbridge crossing Panchuela Creek. Cave Creek Trail 288, which accesses the Dockweiler Trail, begins here.

The hike: Although this is not a hike with spectacular vistas, it has its own rewards. We refer to this hike as an "aspen lover's dream," as the trees seem to envelope the entire trail. The hike is also replete with wildflowers, especially in early summer. This hike will be a fee area in 1999, but at the publication of this book the fee was unestablished.

Follow the trail upstream to the left (northwest). The

Dockweiler Trail

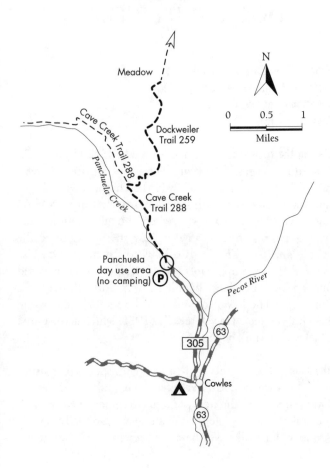

old, large Douglas-firs along the trail are impressive as are the wildflowers such as wild iris, bluebell, wild geranium, and shooting star, growing in early summer. The trail parallels the creek, rises above it, and at approximately 0.8 mile reaches the junction with Dockweiler Trail 259. Turn right (north) onto Dockweiler and begin an ascent on a series of steep switchbacks.

When you reach the top of the ridge the trail levels out for a short time in an aspen and conifer forest. Switchbacks begin again, however, as you follow Jack's Creek drainage to your right (east). When you reach the top of yet another ridge, you will enter a level aspen forest. It is easy to imagine this hike in fall foliage, but we hiked the entire 6 miles in a mid-July thunderstorm. There are more gentle ascents and level areas as you continue to head north through large stands of aspen.

The turn-around point of this hike is indicated by a large meadow to the left (northwest) of the trail. Aspens surround you as you stand among green grasses and wildflowers. To return retrace your steps back to the trailhead.

15
BEATTY'S FLATS FROM JACK'S CREEK CAMPGROUND

Type of hike: Out-and-back.
Distance: 13 miles, round trip.
Elevaton gain: 1,800 feet to Beatty's Flats.
Maps: Elk Mountain (USGS), Pecos Falls (USGS), Cowles (USGS), Pecos Wilderness (USFS).

Finding the trailhead: From Santa Fe take U.S. Highway 25 toward Las Vegas. Take Exit 299 for New Mexico Highway 50, Glorieta, and Pecos. Follow NM 50 to the town of Pecos and the intersection with NM 63. Turn left onto NM 63 and drive through Terrero and Cowles. Jack's Campground is 2.3 miles beyond Cowles on NM 63. When you reach the campground, turn right into the wilderness parking and equestrian camping area. There is a $2 per day charge for parking. The trailhead for Trail 25 lies to the left (north) of the Pecos Wilderness map and information board.

The hike: The destination for this hike is the location of an old cabin that no longer exists; it was built by a gold miner in the late 1800s. It is still sometimes referred to as Beatty's Cabin and is located near the confluence of the Pecos River and Rito del Padre. This area is often called the heart of the Pecos Wilderness because it is accessible by a large number of hiking trails.

Beatty's Flats from Jack's Creek Campground

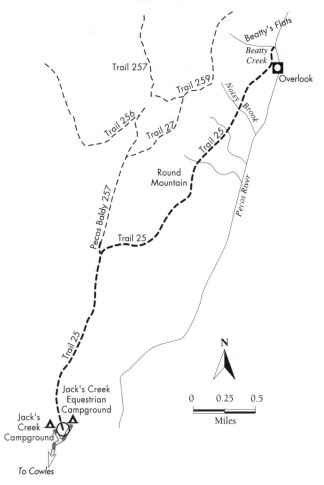

The trailhead for Trail 25 is adjacent to equestrian facilities; therefore, it is a popular horse trail and can become extremely muddy and difficult to maneuver in rainy weather.

The options given are all for moderate hikes continuing along the same trail and differ only in distance. Let stamina, motivation, and time restraints guide your selection.

The trail heads north with a gradual ascent among aspen, ponderosa pine, Gambel oak, and Douglas-fir. It begins to gain greater elevation in a long series of switchbacks. On one of the latter turns a wooden fence and gate appear on the right; be certain to stay on the main trail, turning left (north). After the trail levels out at the top of the ridge there is one more short climb before you are in a vast open meadow dotted here and there with dark areas of aspens and mixed conifers. At approximately 2 miles a trail marker indicates that Beatty's Trail 25 forks right (northeast) and Pecos Baldy Lake Trail 257 turns to the left (northwest). Continue following Trail 25.

Although the trail gradually gains elevation as it skirts the east side of Round Mountain, this is a pleasant meadow hike with several small creek crossings. Wildflowers are plentiful, and there are large white and subalpine firs as well as groves of aspens along the trail, which you may be sharing with grazing cattle.

After leaving the meadow, the trail makes a long, gradual descent to the Pecos River. There are several stream crossings and, true to its name, Noisy Brook seems to be the loudest and can be heard a good distance away. It is the largest of the streams, with a single log holding back the flow of water, creating a small, sandy pool. This is a fine resting spot and perhaps turn-around place, too.

If you continue, the trail quickly takes you to an open meadow with an excellent view of Hamilton Mesa to the right (east) before it descends through alternating conifer and aspen forests. Cow parsnip seems to be growing everywhere. Approximately 1.5 miles from Noisy Brook a rock outcrop and large clearing appear to the right (east) of the trail. This is an overlook for the Pecos River Gorge and another place to either explore or rest. A wonderful view of the meadows at Beatty's lies to the north, and should you choose to go on, there is one final descent to the flats area. Camping and fires are prohibited at Beatty's Flats.

Retrace your route for your return. When you are nearing the last leg of the hike, before leaving the meadow, you will find a most spectacular panoramic view of Santa Fe Baldy and Lake and Penitente Peaks to the southwest. A welcome descent takes you back to the trailhead.

16
BEATTY'S FLATS FROM IRON GATE CAMPGROUND

Type of hike: Out-and-back.
Distance: 11 miles, round trip.
Elevaton gain: 1,640 feet.
Maps: Elk Mountain (USGS), Pecos Falls (USGS), Pecos Wilderness (USFS).

Finding the trailhead: From Santa Fe take U.S. Highway 25 toward Las Vegas. Take Exit 299 to New Mexico Highway 50, Glorieta, and Pecos. Follow NM 50 to the town of Pecos and the intersection with NM 63. Turn left onto NM 63 and drive through the small town of Terrero, consisting of a small grocery store-post office combination and a few homes. Approximately 5 miles beyond Terrero is a right-hand (east) turn for Iron Gate Campground. The dirt road leading to the campground is approximately 4 miles long, often steep, with several deep ditches. We recommend that you drive a high-clearance vehicle and use this trailhead only during dry weather because rain or snow would only intensify an already troublesome situation.

The trailhead for Hamilton Mesa 249 is located at the far (northeast) end of the campground, and there are parking spaces for hikers nearby.

The hike: This hike offers spectacular views from Hamilton Mesa of the principal peaks in the Pecos Wilderness. We found many early summer wildflowers throughout the hike, but the most

Beatty's Flats from Iron Gate Campground

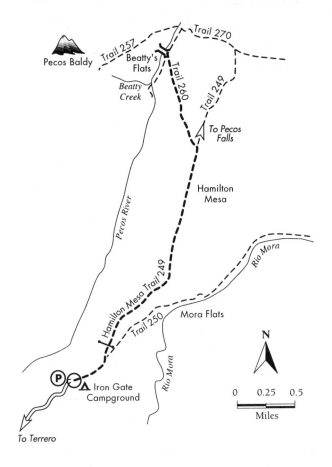

Pecos Baldy

Trail 257

Trail 270

Beatty's Flats

Trail 260

Trail 249

Beatty Creek

To Pecos Falls

Pecos River

Hamilton Mesa

Hamilton Mesa Trail 249

Rio Mora

Trail 250

Mora Flats

N

Rio Mora

P

Iron Gate Campground

0   0.25   0.5

Miles

To Terrero

impressive and abundant were the wild iris or Rocky Mountain flag. Iron Gate Campground will be a fee area in 1999, but as of this guide's publication the fees were undetermined.

To begin this hike leave the campground through the iron gate; the well-worn trail heads east and gently climbs to the ridge above the Mora River. It doesn't take long to discover that this is a trail well used by horses. At the top of the ridge there are several smaller trails leading to views of the Rio Mora Canyon to the right (east); however, to continue walk left (north) along the ridge until you reach a trail junction (about 1 mile from the trailhead) of Hamilton Mesa Trail 249 heading to the left (northwest) and Rociada Trail 250 heading to Mora Flats. Follow Trail 249, which gradually ascends to a gate through which you must pass and then, at approximately 2 miles, brings you to the beautiful, open meadow of Hamilton Mesa. To the left (northwest) you can see Pecos Baldy; midway through your walk on the mesa, views open up of Truchas Peak, Santa Fe Baldy, and Penitente and Lake Peaks. Patches of conifer forest appear here and there to add diversity to the gentle meadow landscape.

At 3.5 miles Trail 260 to Beatty's branches off to the left (northwest) and Trail 249 continues straight ahead to Pecos Falls. As you turn onto Trail 260, you will almost immediately enter a conifer forest and begin the downhill hike to the Pecos River and Beatty's. After hiking approximately 1 mile on Trail 260, another gate appears and a sign indicates that Beatty's is 0.5 mile to the left (northwest). The Pecos River is soon audible below, and when you reach it a sturdy bridge will take you to the meadow on the opposite side. This is the place to rest and relax before retracing your steps back to the trailhead.

17
STEWART LAKE

Type of hike: Out-and-back.
Distance: 11.5 miles, round trip.
Elevaton gain: 2,000 feet.
Maps: Pecos Wilderness (USFS).

Finding the trailhead: From Santa Fe take U.S. Highway 25 toward Las Vegas. Take Exit 299 to New Mexico Highway 50, Glorieta, and Pecos. Follow NM 50 to the town of Pecos and the intersection with NM 63. Turn left onto NM 63 and drive 20 miles to the small community of Cowles. When you see the bridge crossing the Pecos River turn left (west) and park to your immediate right (north) before crossing the bridge. Walk across the bridge and up the hill to your right (north) to the Pecos Wilderness map and sign-in station.

The hike: Although this hike, which uses Winsor Ridge Trail 271, is not steep, it has a gradual ascent the entire length and can be taxing. It may be wise to get some experience and build stamina on shorter trails before attempting Stewart Lake. This hike is popular for horses and anglers, as the lake is known to hold brown, cutthroat, and rainbow trout. An important consideration when hiking this trail in summer is effective bug repellent. We forgot ours and resorted to borrowing from fellow hikers.

The hike begins on a narrow trail to the left of the map

Stewart Lake

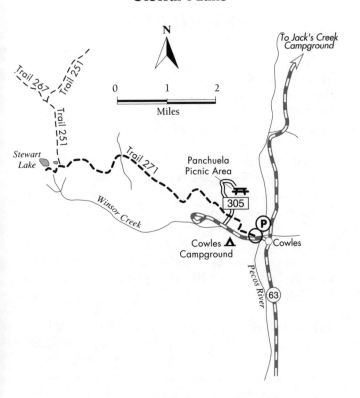

and sign-in area and proceeds uphill, crossing the paved road that leads to Panchuela Day Use Area. Continue climbing to the northwest; the trail then turns to the west. After a short walk you will come upon a sign indicating Winsor

Ridge Trail 271 to Stewart Lake, straight ahead 5.8 miles. Gambel oak, ponderosa pine, and aspen predominate as you continue your ascent on the ridge.

Winsor Creek and many private summer homes can be seen to your left (south) as you hike out of the canyon floor. Switchbacks begin about 0.8 mile. About 3 miles into the hike the trail appears to fork. Stay to the left (west), crossing a muddy creek surrounded by cow parsnip.

The trail continues with gradual ups and downs until you make a final descent and reach a trail marker for Skyline Trail 251. Stewart Lake is to your left (south), about half a mile from this point. As the trail continues it crosses a small stream and skirts a lovely pond surrounded by marshlands. Stewart Lake is a short walk ahead at the top of a small rise and ringed by a well-worn trail. Enjoy a rest or try your hand at trout fishing and then retrace your steps on a downhill trek back to the trailhead.

18
JACK'S CREEK

Type of hike: Out-and-back.
Distance: 9 miles, round trip.
Elevaton gain: 1,550 feet.
Maps: Cowles (USGS), Truchas (USGS).

Finding the trailhead: From Santa Fe take U.S. Highway 25 Las Vegas. Take Exit 299 for New Mexico Highway 50, Glorieta, and Pecos. Follow NM 50 to the town of Pecos and the intersection with NM 63. Turn left onto NM 63 and drive through the communities of Terrero and Cowles. Jack's Creek Campground is 2.3 miles beyond Cowles on NM 63. When you reach the campground, turn right into the wilderness parking and equestrian camping area. There is a $2 per day charge for parking. The trailhead for Trail 25 lies to the left (north) of the Pecos Wilderness map and information board.

The hike: This is a hike filled with wonderful distant views of the high Pecos Wilderness peaks. Be sure to carry alot of film in your backpack. If you decide to spend several days exploring this area, Jack's Creek campground, the originating point of the hike, is located in a beautiful aspen meadow and is a great place to stay. Keep in mind that fires and camping are not allowed within 200 feet of Pecos Baldy Lake.

The trail heads north with a gradual ascent among aspen, ponderosa pine, Gambel oak and Douglas fir before it

Jack's Creek

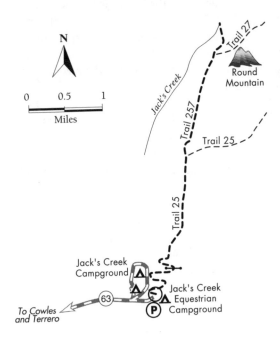

begins to gain greater elevation in a long series of switchbacks. On one of the latter turns, a wooden fence and gate appear on the right; be certain to stay on the main trail, turning left (north). After the trail levels out at the top of the ridge there is one more short climb before you are in a vast, open meadow dotted here and there with dark areas of aspens and mixed conifers.

At approximately 2 miles you will come to the junction of Trail 25, continuing east to Beatty's and Trail 257. Take 257 left (northwest) to Pecos Baldy Lake. You will find beautiful meadows with wild iris, aspen groves, and an occasional large Douglas-fir surrounding the west side of Round Mountain. This is a great destination for a short day hike, as you already have wonderful views of Pecos Baldy ahead of you (northwest) and Redondo Peak and Santa Fe Baldy due west.

If you continue another 2 miles, you will hike past Round Mountain and reach Jack's Creek, another good turnaround point for a day hike.

Bandelier National Monument

Located 48 miles northwest of Santa Fe, Bandelier has 70 miles of hiking trails in what is known to be one of the most archaeologically rich sites in the Unites States. The drive from Santa Fe presents many opportunities for exploration in the nearby pueblos of Tesuque, Santa Clara, or San Ildefonso, where you can get a close view of Black Mesa, the site in 1692 of the reconquest of New Mexico by Spanish forces. Presently it is held sacred by the Pueblo peoples nearby and closed to hiking. As you ascend out of the valley floor on your drive west, keep your eyes peeled for ancient cliff dwellings. There is evidence that people arrived here about 10,000 years ago, but the cliffs were here long before, reminders of the volcanic activity millions of years ago.

There are more than 1,000 ruins within the 50 square miles of Bandelier National Monument, with a series of well-maintained trails leading to many of these ancient sites. "The ancient ones" or Anasazi arrived in Frijoles Canyon about A.D. 950 and flourished until about 1550. Their disappearance from Bandelier as well as from numerous other locations in New Mexico still mystifies the scientific community.

Many hikes begin at the extremely informative Bandelier visitor center and focus on the Frijoles Canyon cliff dwellings nearby. There is some wheelchair accessibility on these trails. Other hikes are longer, begin at different areas of the park, and highlight the geological features of the area as well as the breathtaking scenery. The main area closes at dusk, so plan accordingly if starting a late afternoon excursion.

Tsankawi is a separate, unexcavated section of the monument located near White Rock, 11 miles north of the main entrance. A 1.5-mile-loop trail, often in the actual footsteps of prehistoric dwellers of this area, offers a glimpse into life on this plateau and features a large ruin, cave dwellings, and numerous petroglyphs.

A word of caution when hiking in Bandelier: Prepare for hot summer hiking by carrying lots of water, sunscreen, and a hat!

A wonderful campground lies close to the entrance of Bandelier, and, when trying to make reservations, we were told that in 10 years it has never been filled to capacity!

19
FREY TRAIL

Type of hike: Out-and-back.
Distance: 4 miles, round trip.
Elevaton gain: 600 feet.
Maps: Frijoles (USGS), Bandelier National Monument (Trails Illustrated Topo Maps), Hiking Trails and Jeep Roads of Los Alamos County, Bandelier National Monument and Vicinity (Otowi Station Science Museum Shop and Book Store, Los Alamos).

Finding the trailhead: From Santa Fe take U.S. Highway 285 and US 84 north to Pojoaque. At Pojoaque take New Mexico Highway 502 west, following signs for Los Alamos. Follow NM 502 for approximately 12 miles to the junction with New Mexico 4. Following signs for Bandelier National Monument and White Rock, take NM 4 south for approximately 25 miles to Bandelier National Monument. Turn left (south) into the monument entrance, where you will pay a fee of $10, which is good for the whole week.

Follow the road a short distance until you see the signs for Juniper Campground. Turn right (west), driving past the campground registration booth, until you see signs for amphitheater parking on your left. The trailhead is clearly marked and is located in the southwest corner of the lot. Frijoles Canyon ruins are 1.6 miles from this point, and the visitor center is 2 miles. No dogs or bikes are allowed on this trail.

Frey Trail

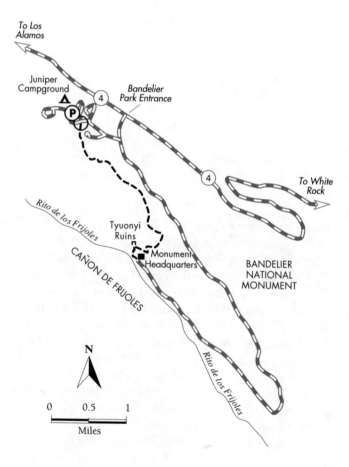

To Los
Alamos

Juniper
Campground

*Bandelier
Park Entrance*

4

P

4

To White
Rock

Rito de los Frijoles

Tyuonyi
Ruins

Monument
Headquarters

CAÑON DE FRIJOLES

BANDELIER
NATIONAL
MONUMENT

Rito de los Frijoles

N

0   0.5   1

Miles

The hike: This hike provides an excellent opportunity within Bandelier National Monument to get an overview of Frijoles Canyon and Tyuonyi Ruin before setting out to explore them in depth. The hike, which ends at park headquarters, is all downhill, and you may want to visit the ruins, museum, bookstore, or gift shop before hiking back uphill to your car. Remember, the monument closes at dusk.

The trail begins by heading southeast from the amphitheater parking lot amid pinyon, juniper, and ponderosa pine. A short distance into the hike you will cross a dirt road and pick up the marked trail on the other side. A gentle descent begins at this point, and you will then cross a second road. The trail continues to your left (east) across the road. Once again, it is well marked. At 0.8 mile is a trail marker indicating that the ruins are 0.6 mile and the visitor center 1.2 miles.

At approximately 1 mile you have a spectacular view of the canyon and the ruins to the east. A series of gradually descending switchbacks takes you to the bottom of the canyon. When you come to the first fork in the trail take a right (west) and at the next fork turn to your left (west), following the sign to the visitor center. You will walk through the Tyuonyi Ruins but may want to return with the self-guided pamphlet available at the center. In addition to exploring park headquarters and hiking the main ruins on the canyon floor, you may wish to visit the Ceremonial Cave with its restored kiva, an easy 2-mile hike up Frijoles Canyon. Be sure to save some energy for the 600-foot ascent back to the amphitheater trailhead.

20
CAÑON DE VALLE

Type of hike: Out-and-back.
Distance: 6 miles, round trip.
Elevaton gain: 1,200 feet.
Maps: Frijoles (USGS), Bland (USGS), Hiking Trails and Jeep Road of Los Alamos County, Bandelier National Monument and Vicinity (Otowi Station Science Museum Shop and Book Store, Los Alamos), Santa Fe National Forest (USFS).

Finding the trailhead: From Santa Fe take U.S. Highway 285 and US 84 north to Pojoaque. At Pojoaque take New Mexico Highway 502 west, following signs to Los Alamos, approximately 12 miles to the junction with New Mexico Highway 4. Follow NM 4 for approximately 31 miles (passing the entrance to Bandelier National Monument) to the intersection of NM 501. Turn right (north) and drive 1.3 miles, then turn left (west) onto dirt road 2996 and into a small parking area. The trailhead for Cañon de Valle, Trail 289, lies to the southwest past a metal gate and fence.

The hike: Although there is a substantial elevation gain on this hike, it is for the most part a pleasant, gentle trail along the canyon bottom, paralleling a small stream. We met a friendly hiking group from Los Alamos and two mountain bikers; however, the appearance of the trail indicated little use.

The first portion of this hike is along a wide, rocky, seldom-used road lined with ponderosa pine, Gambel oak, and mixed conifers. After about 0.8 mile continue straight ahead (northwest) on a nar-

Cañon De Valle

SANTA FE NATIONAL FOREST

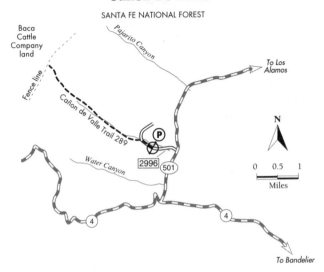

row trail while the road ascends to the right (north). You will begin a gradual ascent as the trail widens then narrows again. Several easy creek crossings and the lush riparian vegetation make this section of the hike, along the bottom of the canyon, pleasant, cool, and interesting. After about 2 miles a steeper ascent begins on the northeast side of the canyon, and you lose the stream with the higher ground.

The trail's end is marked by three metal poles immediately followed by a barbed-wire fence. This is the property boundary for the Baca Cattle Company. The Baca family once owned most of the surrounding land, including the Valle Grande, one of the largest volcanic calderas in the world, encompassing approximately 176 square miles. There is no trespassing beyond this point. Your return to the trailhead is an easy downhill trek.

21
FALLS TRAIL

Type of hike: Out-and-back.
Distance: 5 miles, round trip.
Elevaton gain: 700 feet.
Maps: Frijoles (USGS), Bandelier National Monument (Trails Illustrated Topo Maps), Hiking Trails and Jeep Roads of Los Alamos County, Bandelier National Monument and Vicinity (Otowi Station Science Museum Shop and Book Store, Los Alamos).

Finding the trailhead: From Santa Fe take U.S. Highway 285 and US 84 north to Pojoaque. At Pojoaque take New Mexico Highway 502 west, following signs to Los Alamos, for approximately 12 miles, to the junction with New Mexico 4. Take NM 4 south to Bandelier National Monument, approximately 25 miles. Turn left into the monument entrance, where you pay a fee of $10, which is good for the whole week. Follow the road for about 3 miles to park headquarters, cross the bridge at the end of the parking lot, and look for designated backcountry parking to your left. The trailhead is at the far (south) end of the parking lot.

The hike: This hike provides an opportunity to see not only the natural beauty of the falls but also the geological history and vegetative diversity present in Frijoles Canyon. You will pass two waterfalls on your way to the Rio Grande. The

Falls Trail

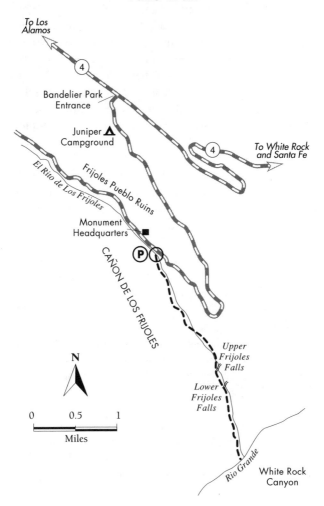

To Los Alamos

4

Bandelier Park Entrance

Juniper Campground

4

To White Rock and Santa Fe

El Rito de Los Frijoles

Frijoles Pueblo Ruins

Monument Headquarters

P

CAÑON DE LOS FRIJOLES

N

0   0.5   1

Miles

Upper Frijoles Falls

Lower Frijoles Falls

Rio Grande

White Rock Canyon

71

hike begins close to the monument bookstore and museum, giving you the opportunity to pick up a self-guide pamphlet for the trail, "A Guide to Falls Trail, Bandelier National Monument." It is an excellent source for detailed information on the geology of the entire Jemez Mountain area. You may want to hike some of the other trails of Bandelier and do a little shopping at the gift shop, which has a fine selection of Native American art from the surrounding pueblos. When planning this hike keep in mind that the monument closes at dusk.

A marker at the trailhead indicates that Upper Falls is 1.5 miles, Lower Falls is 2 miles, and the Rio Grande is 2.5 miles (elevation change of 700 feet). The wide, well-maintained and well-used path winds along, near, and beside El Rito de los Frijoles (Little River of the Beans) and through a juniper and large ponderosa pine forest.

After approximately a mile you will begin your descent into the canyon. Bordering the trail are tent rocks, eroded columns of volcanic rock (tuff) that were escape routes for hot gases millions of years ago. Also notice the tuff cliffs above you as you approach the stream. Several sturdy wooden bridges in this area make creek crossings easy, and the vegetation is wonderfully varied as you walk closer to the falls. Our most interesting find for the day was the large banana yucca with its fat, bananalike fruit.

The overlook at the falls affords you a view not only of the waterfall but also of the canyon's unique geology. You will now enter the bottom of the canyon and may notice that the stream that was next to you is now far below. Look back to see the second falls behind you.

As you continue to follow the trail leading to the Rio Grande, you will encounter many stream crossings and many ancillary trails, which eventually all connect with the main trail again. The last portion of the trail takes you into a tree-less, wide-open area that is the result of unusually high run-off and flooding from the Cochiti Dam in 1985. The abundance of dead juniper provides an excellent habitat for many birds, including swallows and mountain bluebirds. You may notice canyon grape, another unusual plant. To reach the water's edge, look for a large snag to the left (east) and the trail leading to it. The sandy beach here is a great place to enjoy the Rio Grande before retracing your route uphill to the trailhead. Keep in mind the monument closes at dusk.

Los Alamos

Hiking in this area of northern New Mexico is more remote and less populated with hikers than those trails closer to Santa Fe. Whether you are hiking in Bandelier, White Rock, or closer to Los Alamos, a trip into this once secret city is highly encouraged. The Bradbury Science Museum located on Central Avenue in Los Alamos offers a detailed history of the Manhattan Project as well as many hands-on exhibits that explain the current work of the Los Alamos National Laboratory. The short film depicting the founding of this unusual city is especially interesting and informative.

A short drive west on Central Avenue brings you to the Fuller Lodge Complex. This beautiful log structure was the center of activity for the prestigious boarding school and later became the focal point of the atomic city. Here you will also find the Los Alamos Historical Museum and Book Shop, offering a wonderful miniview of the history of the Pajarito Plateau as well as other exhibits and memorabilia from the early days of Los Alamos. A drive around Los Alamos, with its interconnecting plateaus and varied forms of construction, reveals the history of a city built quickly and in secrecy.

Visit the Los Alamos County Chamber of Commerce and White Rock Tourist Information Center for information regarding other hiking trails in this area. Be aware that many inviting canyon and mesa areas belonging to LANL (Los Alamos National Laboratory) are closed to all trespassing and are marked accordingly.

Caution: When hiking in summer, weather is often dry and hot. Bring lots of water, sunscreen, and a hat. Check specific hikes for recommendations as to weather precautions.

22
GUAJE TRAIL

Type of hike: Out-and-back.
Distance: 6 miles, one way.
Elevaton gain: 1,200 feet.
Maps: Valle Toledo (USGS), Hiking Trails and Jeep Roads of Los Alamos County, Bandelier National Monument and Vicinity (Otowi Station Science Museum Shop and Book Store, Los Alamos), Santa Fe National Forest (USFS).

Finding the trailhead: From Santa Fe take U.S. Highway 285 and US 84 north to Pojoaque. At Pojoaque take New Mexico Highway 502 west, following signs for Los Alamos, approximately 12 miles, to the junction with NM 4. Take NM 4 west, following the signs for White Rock and Bandelier. At 1.4 miles take NM 501 right (north) on East Jemez Road (the truck route) to Los Alamos. You will see the Los Alamos National Laboratory to your left. Go straight through the intersection with Diamond Drive, and approximately 1.5 miles from this intersection look for the sign for Pajarito Ski Area to your right (east). Turn and drive for approximately 4 miles to the ski hill. Park at the far (west) end of the parking lot and walk a short distance to a dirt road on the right (north) where you will see a trail marker for Guaje Canyon Trail 282.

The hike: This hike is called the Quemason Trail on the Hiking Trails and Jeep Roads of Los Alamos County map. It

Guaje Trail

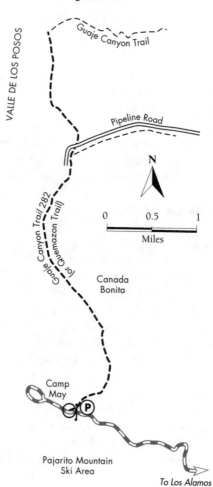

Guaje Canyon Trail

VALLE DE LOS POSOS

Pipeline Road

N

0   0.5   1
Miles

Guaje Canyon Trail 282
(or Quemazon Trail)

Canada
Bonita

SIERRA DE LOS VALLES

Camp
May

P

Pajarito Mountain
Ski Area

To Los Alamos

begins north of Los Alamos at Pajarito Ski Area and gives an easy introduction to the gentle and inviting Jemez Mountains. In addition, the beautiful meadow Canada Bonita lies directly in your path. The route from Santa Fe takes you through the city of Los Alamos, where you may want to spend time learning the history of this once secret city.

Guaje trail heads east on the dirt road, and you are immediately confronted with a metal gate to go through or around. You will pass several cross-country ski trails, but stay on the main trail. At approximately 1 mile, after a series of gradual ascents and descents, you will come to a large meadow called Canada Bonita ("pretty watercourse"), a USDA Forest Service Research Natural Area, protected because of its unique montane grassland. The trail skirts the south end of the meadow and then turns north where there is a wonderful view of the Rio Grande valley to the southeast. As you ascend through aspen trees the trail reaches its highest elevation, 9,540 feet.

Continue walking to a second metal gate, at which point Guaje Trail joins Pipeline Road. Walk straight ahead to a sign marking Guaje Canyon Trail to the left (northwest). Pipeline Road continues to the right (northeast). You may wish to follow Guaje Canyon Trail for a short time, as it offers beautiful vistas of the valley to your left (west). Simply retrace your steps in order to return to the trailhead and the ski area.

23
ANCHO RAPIDS

Type of hike: Out-and-back.
Distance: 6 miles, round trip.
Elevaton gain: 1,230 feet.
Maps: White Rock (USGS) (trail not identified), Santa Fe National Forest (USFS) (trail not identified), Hiking Trails and Jeep Roads of Los Alamos County, Bandelier National Monument and Vicinity (Otowi Station Science Museum Shop and Book Store, Los Alamos) (trail not identified).

Finding the trailhead: From Santa Fe, take U.S. Highway 285 and US 84 north to Pojoaque. At Pojoaque take New Mexico Highway 502 west, following signs for Los Alamos, for approximately 12 miles, until you reach the intersection with NM 4. Follow NM 4 south into White Rock. After the first traffic light, the visitor's center can be seen on the right. Set your odometer at this point. You will come to the trailhead in 3.9 miles. As you drive along NM 4 notice the gates, giving access to the canyons on the south side of the highway, positioned at intervals on your left. As you leave White Rock the gate numbers become smaller. You are looking for gate 4 (the trailhead) and the small gravel parking area in front of it.

The hike: This is a desert plateau and canyon hike to the Rio Grande. After an easy beginning on high desert terrain, the trail descends along switchbacks, through a small, lush riparian area, onto the sandy banks and smooth black boulders bordering the Rio Grande. There is no shade on this hike, and in the heat of summer it could be a scorcher, so it may be a good idea to wait for a cool day. It is also an isolated hike. We saw no one and appreciated each other's company.

The trail begins on a very flat dirt road, constructed for the powerlines under which you will walk. Notice the wonderful views of the Rio Grande valley, Sangre de Cristo Mountains (we saw them with a dusting of snow in early June), and the Sandia Mountains near Albuquerque (beyond the big white satellite dish belonging to Los Alamos National Laboratory). If hiking in early summer, you may want to get some close-up photographs of the bright yellow prickly pear cacti that flourish in the desert sand.

Continue walking on the road adjacent to the powerline towers and at 1.8 miles (between the fifth and sixth towers) take a small cutoff to your right (southeast). After about .25 mile this road ends. Veer to the left (south) up a slight incline, and then look to your right to find cairns leading to an old fence and gate guarding the rim of Ancho Canyon. Walk to the right (southeast) of the fence and follow the path through the pink sandstone cliffs, where you begin your descent into the canyon.

The expansive view from the boulders on the edge of the canyon shows you the trail below, meandering along through the dry canyon, through a lush riparian area, and eventually to the river. A long series of switchbacks, with more great photo opportunities, brings you to the bottom of the canyon (in early summer the cholla cacti are in bloom along this descent). Again, look for the cairns to guide you

Ancho Rapids

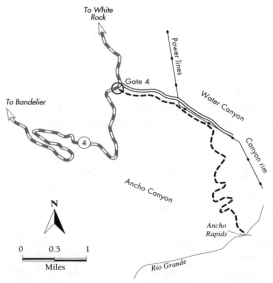

To White Rock

Power lines

Gate 4

Water Canyon

To Bandelier

Canyon rim

4

Ancho Canyon

N

Ancho Rapids

0   0.5   1

Miles

Rio Grande

along the path on the canyon bottom; the vegetation changes and becomes more varied as you approach the spring. Follow the spring south, along one of the many trails paralleling it, to the Rio Grande. The rewards are great—a wonderful sandy beach with beautiful black boulders you can rest on or climb as Ancho Rapids roars in front of you.

The only damper on your relaxation may be the anticipation of the hike back. You can easily locate the return trail by looking back up the canyon to your starting place, which is marked with a big splash of white, at the edge of the cliffs. This marks your path as you retrace your steps up the canyon and then hike back to gate 4 and your car.

24
APACHE SPRINGS

Type of hike: Loop.
Distance: 9.5 miles, round trip.
Elevaton gain: 1,410 feet.
Maps: Frijoles (USGS), Bandelier National Monument (Trails Illustrated Topo Maps), Hiking Trails and Jeep Roads of Los Alamos County, Bandelier National Monument and Vicinity (Otowi Station Science Museum Shop and Book Store, Los Alamos).

Finding the trailhead: From Santa Fe drive north on U.S. Highway 285 and US 84 north to Pojoaque. At Pojoaque take New Mexico Highway 502 west, following signs for Los Alamos. Follow NM 502 for approximately 12 miles to the intersection of NM 4. Drive south on NM 4, following signs for White Rock and Bandelier National Monument, for about 32.2 miles. En route you will pass the Bandelier entrance at approximately 25 miles (the trailhead is 7.2 miles beyond this entrance). You will then pass the junction with NM 501 and the old "back gate" still intact from the years when Los Alamos was a closed city. Continue straight ahead on NM 4. The trailhead can be identified by a small parking lot and a gate numbered 10 on the left (south) side of the road. Beyond the gate is a Bandelier National Monument sign, with its characteristic turkeys, marking the beginning of Apache Springs Trail.

Apache Springs

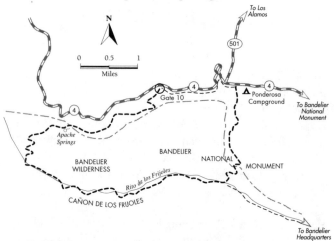

The hike: This hike takes you into the Bandelier Wilderness to experience quite a different environment from the summer crowds and activity centering around Bandelier Park Headquarters. We found steep descents and ascents, rare wildflowers, and welcoming Frijoles Creek—all in all a great day hike!

From the trailhead an old logging road takes you south through a forest of Gambel oak, ponderosa pine, and aspen. Among the wildflowers in bloom along the trail in July were beautiful bright red skyrocket penstamen. The trail quickly cuts through a meadow and gently ascends a ridge where you will find a sign for Apache Springs to the right (southwest). The next portion of the hike cuts through the La Mesa burn of 1977. New Mexican locust and aspen line the trail, and evidence of new growth is everywhere.

At about 1.3 miles you will come to the rim of Frijoles Canyon and the Bandelier Wilderness boundary. A trail marker indicates that Apache Springs is 0.1 mile, Beaver Dam 2 miles, and Upper Crossing 5.1 miles. Descend to the right (southwest) into the canyon. At the bottom a sign signifies Apache Springs to your left (east). The actual spring is just a short distance from this point and is encased in concrete and stone. It was once used as a watering hole for cows and sheep on their way to summer pasture in the Valle Grande.

To continue, return to the sign and follow the trail west, as it climbs up and out of the canyon. Be sure to stay on the main trail, and at about 2 miles you will reach the rim of Frijoles Canyon. The trail leads to the right (southwest), and you descend 800 feet to the canyon bottom on rocky, steep switchbacks. Unusual volcanic rock formations can be seen across the canyon, to the south. Frijoles Creek awaits you at the end of this difficult (and potentially hot) 0.5-mile descent. After an easy crossing on rocks the trail heads left (east), paralleling the creek. In late July this was a hot and humid but level part of the hike. We felt fortunate to find the endangered Rocky Mountain lily in bloom; however, we also found stinging nettles and poison ivy, so beware.

After about 3 miles, a trail marker points the way to Ponderosa Campground (your destination), 1.5 miles and a 450-foot climb. Follow the trail across a footbridge to the left (north) and up a series of switchbacks (we counted 13). The trail gradually works its way through a ponderosa forest, and shortly before the end of the hike the trail you come to a T where you will turn left (north) and continue on through the campground to NM 4. Walk 1.7 miles on the highway (unfortunately uphill) back to the trailhead and your car.

25
MITCHELL TRAIL

Type of hike: Out-and-back.
Distance: 5.5 miles, round trip.
Elevaton gain: 1,160 feet.
Maps: Guaje Mountain (USGS), Hiking Trails and Jeep Roads of Los Alamos County, Bandelier National Monument and Vicinity (Otowi Station Science Museum Shop and Book Store, Los Alamos), Santa Fe National Forest (USFS).

Finding the trailhead: From Santa Fe take U.S. Highway 285 and US 84 north to Pojoaque. At Pojoaque take New Mexico Highway 502 west, following signs for Los Alamos. Stay on NM 502 and you will enter the city up a series of switchbacks and past the old main gate, where all residents were required to show badges in order to enter the city in the "secret years". Follow Trinity Drive through the center of town until it intersects with Diamond Drive. Turn right (north) on Diamond Drive and follow it approximately 2.5 miles to 36th Street. Turn left (west) on 36th and follow it until it intersects with Arizona Street. Again turn left (west); the two-car trailhead parking is approximately 0.3 mile on your right, at the corner of Arizona and 45th Street. The spot is also marked with a Forest Service sign.

The hike: This hike begins in a residential area in Los Alamos. To reach the trailhead you must go through the community

Mitchell Trail

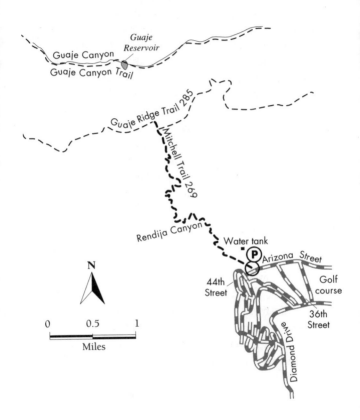

Guaje Canyon

Guaje Reservoir

Guaje Canyon Trail

Guaje Ridge Trail 285

Mitchell Trail 269

Rendija Canyon

Water tank

P

Arizona Street

Golf course

44th Street

36th Street

Diamond Drive

N

0   0.5   1

Miles

center where two excellent museums are located. You may want to plan extra time for exploring the history of Los Alamos as well as its environs. The hike takes you into the Jemez Mountains. As with other hikes in the Jemez, be aware of late afternoon thunderstorms in July and August. The lightning on the these mountains peaks can be perilous.

The hike begins with an immediate ascent north on a well-worn, rocky trail amid ponderosa pines. In about 200 yards the trail crosses a firebreak road. Keep on the main trail heading northwest, which descends into Rendija Canyon and parallels an ephemeral stream on the canyon floor. Douglas fir, ponderosa pine, and Gambel oak dot a rather dry forest. The trail winds through the canyon with gradual ascents and descents. At about 0.8 mile a trail intersects from the right (north). This is a 0.5-mile trail to a natural arch. If you wish to take this short deviation from the hike, turn and follow the trail uphill, noticing the yellow dots located on trees marking your path. If you continue on the main trail, another fork will appear approximately a mile into the hike. Be certain to stay on the lower, more prominent trail.

The trail traverses the south side of the canyon before dropping down momentarily, then ascending via switchbacks on the north side to the top of the first ridge. This is a good turnaround or resting point. You have hiked 2 miles and gained 950 feet in elevation.

If you continue to the top of the next ridge (0.8 mile, 210 feet elevation gain) you will reach the intersection of Mitchell Trail 269 and Guaje Ridge Trail 285. As you hike, be sure to notice the views of the Rio Grande valley and Sangre de Cristo Mountains to the east. At the intersection of the two trails there is a plaque commemorating the accomplishment of David Mitchell, a young man who, at age 14, built the trail to the Guaje Canyon Reservoir for his Eagle Scout project. This is the turnaround point, although Mitchell Trail does continue into the deep canyon to the north and ends at Guaje Reservoir, built in 1946 to serve the newly created city of Los Alamos.

Follow Mitchell Trail back to Los Alamos, but be aware that toward the end of the hike there are ancillary trails, branching out in many directions. Our best advice is to consult your compass and stay south. If necessary, hike to a high point and look for the water tower that will guide you back to the residential area just north of Arizona Avenue, where you can easily find your way back to the trailhead.

For More Information

Bandelier National Monument, HCR 1, Box 1, Suite 15, Los Alamos, NM 87544 (505) 672-3861

The DOME 3801-A Arkansas Avenue, Los Alamos, NM 87544 (505) 661-DOME

The Insiders' Guide to Santa Fe. A. Hillerman and T. Stieber. Falcon Publishing.

Hyde Memorial State Park, 740 Hyde Park Rd, Santa Fe, NM 87501 (505) 983-7175

Los Alamos County Chamber of Commerce, P.O. Box 460VG, Los Alamos, NM (505) 662-8105

New Mexico Public Lands Information Center, 1474 Rodeo Road, P.O. Box 27115, Santa Fe, NM 87502-0115, www.publiclandsinfo.org

New Mexico State Parks Division, P.O. Box 1147, Santa Fe, NM 87505 (505) 827-7173

Santa Fe National Forest, 1474 Rodeo Road, P.O. Box 1689, Santa Fe, NM 87504 Santa Fe Headquarters (505) 438-7840

Pecos Ranger Station (505) 757-6121

Los Alamos Ranger Station (505) 667-5120

Santa Fe Ski Area, 1210 Luisa Street, Suite #5, Santa Fe, NM 87501 (505) 982-9155

U.S. Geological Survey Topographic Maps, Building 41-Denver Federal

Center, Denver, CO 80225 (800) USA-MAPS

U.S. National Forest Reservation Center, P.O. Box 900, Cumberland, MD 21501-0900 1-800-280-CAMP

About the Authors

Katie and Linda both live in Montana and love hiking together. Linda was raised in northern New Mexico and Katie in Montana, where she now works in fish and wildlife management. They are wilderness enthusiasts and have great concerns about its preservation for the future. Both devote time and energy volunteering on environmental and conservation issues.